D1361497

Winter

Julie Murray

Abdo
SEASONS
Kids

abdopublishing.com

Published by Abdo Kids, a division of ABDO, PO Box 398166, Minneapolis, Minnesota 55439.
Copyright © 2016 by Abdo Consulting Group, Inc. International copyrights reserved in all countries.
No part of this book may be reproduced in any form without written permission from the publisher.

Printed in the United States of America, North Mankato, Minnesota.

052015

092015

 THIS BOOK CONTAINS
RECYCLED MATERIALS

Photo Credits: iStock, Shutterstock

Production Contributors: Teddy Borth, Jennie Forsberg, Grace Hansen

Design Contributors: Candice Keimig, Dorothy Toth

Library of Congress Control Number: 2014958555

Cataloging-in-Publication Data

Murray, Julie.

 Winter / Julie Murray.

  p. cm. -- (Seasons)

ISBN 978-1-62970-922-2

Includes index.

1. Winter--Juvenile literature. 2. Seasons--Juvenile literature.   I. Title.

508.2--dc23

2014958555

Table of Contents

Winter 4

Winter Fun 22

Glossary. 23

Index 24

Abdo Kids Code. 24

Winter

Winter is one of the four seasons.

Spring

Summer

Winter

Fall

The air is cold in winter.

The days get shorter.

Snow falls.

It covers the ground.

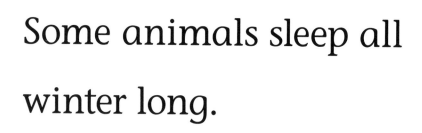

Some animals sleep all winter long.

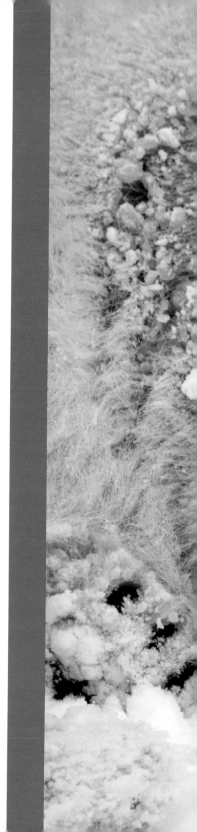

People try to stay **warm**.

They wear hats and mittens.

Winter can be fun!

Sam builds a snowman.

Maria goes sledding.

Tom goes ice skating.

The snow **piles** up high!

Mary helps shovel it.

What will you do this winter?

21

Winter Fun

build a snowman

go sledding

drink hot chocolate

make a snow angel

Glossary

pile
to come together little by little
until there are many in one spot.

warm
a comfortable temperature.

Index

activities 14, 16, 18

animals 10

clothing 12

cold 6

daylight 6

ice skating 16

shovel 18

sledding 16

snow 8, 18

snowman 14

abdokids.com

Use this code to log on to abdokids.com and access crafts, games, videos, and more!

Abdo Kids Code:
SWK9222